theatre & ethics

Theatre &

Series Editors: Jen Harvie and Dan Rebellato

Published

Forthcoming

Theatre& Series
Series Standing Order
ISBN 978-0–230–20327–3

You can receive future titles in this series as they are published by placing a standing order. Please contact your bookseller or, in case of difficulty, write to us at the address below with your name and address, the title of the series and the ISBN quoted above.

Customer Services Department, Macmillan Distribution Ltd
Houndmills, Basingstoke, Hampshire RG21 6XS, England

theatre & ethics

Nicholas Ridout

palgrave
macmillan

First published 2009 by
PALGRAVE MACMILLAN

Palgrave Macmillan in the UK is an imprint of Macmillan Publishers Limited, registered in England, company number 785998, of Houndmills, Basingstoke, Hampshire RG21 6XS.

Palgrave Macmillan in the US is a division of St Martin's Press LLC, 175 Fifth Avenue, New York, NY 10010.

Palgrave Macmillan is the global academic imprint of the above companies and has companies and representatives throughout the world.

Palgrave® and Macmillan® are registered trademarks in the United States, the United Kingdom, Europe and other countries.

ISBN-13: 978–0–230–21027–1 paperback
ISBN-10: 0–230–21027–9 paperback

This book is printed on paper suitable for recycling and made from fully managed and sustained forest sources. Logging, pulping and manufacturing processes are expected to conform to the environmental regulations of the country of origin.

A catalogue record for this book is available from the British Library.

A catalog record for this book is available from the Library of Congress.

10 9 8 7 6 5 4 3 2
18 17 16 15 14 13 12 11 10

Printed and bound in China

contents

series editors' preface

The theatre is everywhere, from entertainment districts to the fringes, from the rituals of government to the ceremony of the courtroom, from the spectacle of the sporting arena to the theatres of war. Across these many forms stretches a theatrical continuum through which cultures both assert and question themselves.

Theatre has been around for thousands of years, and the ways we study it have changed decisively. It's no longer enough to limit our attention to the canon of Western dramatic literature. Theatre has taken its place within a broad spectrum of performance, connecting it with the wider forces of ritual and revolt that thread through so many spheres of human culture. In turn, this has helped make connections across disciplines; over the past fifty years, theatre and performance have been deployed as key metaphors and practices with which to rethink gender, economics, war, language, the fine arts, culture and one's sense of self.

Theatre & is a long series of short books which hopes to capture the restless interdisciplinary energy of theatre and performance. Each book explores connections between theatre and some aspect of the wider world, asking how the theatre might illuminate the world and how the world might illuminate the theatre. Each book is written by a leading theatre scholar and represents the cutting edge of critical thinking in the discipline.

We have been mindful, however, that the philosophical and theoretical complexity of much contemporary academic writing can act as a barrier to a wider readership. A key aim for these books is that they should all be readable in one sitting by anyone with a curiosity about the subject. The books are challenging, pugnacious, visionary sometimes and, above all, clear. We hope you enjoy them.

Jen Harvie and Dan Rebellato

Part One

ancient

How shall I act?

'How shall I act?' That is the question. It is a question
blurted out at a moment of crisis, a question he never
meant to ask, at least not aloud. Neoptolemus, son of the
slain Achilles, is facing an acute ethical problem.

The play is Sophocles' *Philoctetes* (Athens, 409 BCE).
Neoptolemus has been brought by Ulysses from Troy, where
they are both leaders of the Greek army besieging the city,
to the island of Lemnos. They have come to Lemnos because
this is where, years ago, on his way to Troy, Ulysses had
abandoned Philoctetes. Philoctetes, an erstwhile companion
of the demi-god Hercules, had suffered an incurable snake
bite, leaving him with a stinking wound and in intolerable
pain. His cries of pain were damaging morale and interrupt-
ing important sacrificial rituals, and so Ulysses, bowing to
pressure from more powerful Greek leaders, left him on the
deserted island before sailing on to Troy. Unfortunately for

Ulysses and the Greek leaders, however, it turns out that Philoctetes possesses a bow and arrows which, according to prophecy, are the weapons which will secure for the Greeks victory in their war on Troy. So Ulysses has brought young Neoptolemus – a Greek leader whom Philoctetes has never met, and against whom, therefore, he bears no grudge – to entrap Philoctetes and bring him to Troy, where, the Greeks hope, he will use his bow and arrows and bring the war to a successful conclusion.

In the opening scene of the play, as they set foot on the island, Ulysses reveals to Neoptolemus the purpose of their mission. Neoptolemus is to present himself to Philoctetes as a fellow victim of the Greek leadership, with a concocted story about having been deprived by the Greek leaders of his right to his dead father's weapons. Neoptolemus, a young man of virtue, is initially horrified at the proposition that he should lie to obtain Philoctetes' trust: 'Rather, much rather would I fall by virtue / Than rise by guilt to certain victory,' he tells Ulysses (p. 208).

Ulysses, however, soon persuades him, arguing first that the ends (victory over Troy) justify the means (lying to Philoctetes): 'We need not blush at aught / That may promote our interest and success' (p. 210). Ulysses follows this up with the promise that Neoptolemus will win a 'double prize' for going along with his cunning plan: he will gain a reputation for being both 'valiant and wise' (p. 211). This seems to do the trick. Ulysses withdraws and Neoptolemus heads into the interior of the island in search of his stinking, pain-wracked victim.

He soon finds his man and presents his pack of lies. Philoctetes almost inevitably falls for it, expressing passionate sympathy for the young man, who, in his turn, agrees, out of pity for a man so deeply afflicted, to rescue him from the desert island. With bonds of pity and sympathy established, Philoctetes even allows Neoptolemus to take hold of his miraculous bow and arrows. Philoctetes falls into an appalling spasm of renewed agony, as though he were about to die, and it is as he recovers consciousness that Neoptolemus, his hands literally on the prize, experiences his ethical crisis. 'How shall I act?' he asks himself.

One version of ethical thought, held by the Greek philosopher Aristotle, among others, is that ethics rests in the character of an individual. The improvement of your character and the fulfilment of its potential is the aim of ethics, and, indeed, of life itself, according to Aristotle. However, Neoptolemus agreed to go along with Ulysses – against his better judgement, or his sense of his own virtue – because he was persuaded that in doing so he would be serving a higher cause. He might have imagined that he was acting ethically because his action could be defined as seeking the greatest good of the greatest number of people. This is the basis for what is often called 'utilitarian' ethics, generally associated with the English philosopher Jeremy Bentham (1748–1832) and the Scottish philosopher James Mill (1773–1836). Although Neoptolemus might feel uneasy about compromising his character as a man who does not lie, the greater good (victory over Troy) of the greater number (the Greeks as a whole) ought to prevail over his personal sense of virtue.

He might also have been guided by a belief that his actions amounted to the fulfilment of the will of the Gods, made clear in the prophecy that only Philoctetes and his magical bow and arrows would bring about victory over Troy. This would be another kind of ethical argument, in which ethical action consists in following pre-determined rules. In some cultures at some moments in history, ethics has tended to be defined in just these terms: you do as you are told by religious authorities. In some cultures at other moments in history, the belief that you should do as you are told by religious authorities has been challenged. Sometimes the commandments of religion seem to come into conflict with other reasons and desires for action. It is at such moments that an ethical crisis occurs. Sophocles' *Philoctetes* dramatises just such a crisis. Neoptolemus' own ethical judgement seems to be in conflict not only with the judgement of the famously wise (and wily) senior leader Ulysses but also with the will of the Gods.

This situation arises because new sources of ethical judgement have entered the equation, unforeseen by Neoptolemus. At first he seems secure in his ethical stance. He is a man of virtuous character, and men of virtuous character do not tell lies. This position is rapidly undermined, and he proceeds to act in accordance with Ulysses' 'utilitarian' view of ethics (or, one might argue, on the wholly unethical grounds that people will think he is brave and clever if he does so). However, confronted with the pain and suffering of a fellow human being, he experiences such powerful feelings of sympathy that he is moved to act differently, to reveal to Philoctetes the whole plot and to ally himself with Philoctetes against Ulysses.

Neoptolemus, feeling sympathy for his fellow human, may also have started to feel that there is something inherently wrong not just in the act of lying but in the act of using another human being in the way that Ulysses had proposed. Think about Neoptolemus' initial position, in which his ethical stance is determined, or, shall we say, constituted, by his virtuous character. To remain a virtuous character, and thereby preserve his own ethical position, he needs to be in full control of his own actions. He needs to be able to conceive of himself as fully responsible for what he does. If he were somehow tricked into 'acting out of character' and did something that contradicted his sense of his own virtue, he would, justifiably, feel violated, feel that something intrinsic and vital to his sense of who he is had been spoiled or tarnished in some way. He would feel, frankly, 'used'. This is precisely how Philoctetes would feel if he fell for Neoptolemus' lies and surrendered his bow and arrows. He would feel that he had been used as a 'means' to achieve someone else's 'end'. So might Neoptolemus feel, if he stopped to think about how Ulysses had treated him.

No wonder Neoptolemus stops dead in his tracks and asks, 'How shall I act?' It seems as though a whole history of moral philosophy is caught up in this one moment, including moral philosophy from centuries and locations of which neither the fictional character Neoptolemus nor his playwright-creator, Sophocles, would have known anything. 'How shall I act?' is one succinct way of posing the question of ethics. It is also, as you will, of course, have noticed from the very beginning, a theatrical question. In both senses it is a difficult question, and in neither sense is it satisfactorily resolved by the answer that you should 'act better', although this answer is often tempting. The fact that this question can be posed as both ethical and theatrical suggests that there is at least some reason for writing (and reading) a book called *Theatre & Ethics*. As the example from Sophocles' *Philoctetes* shows, at least some theatre appears to dramatise ethical questions, and it therefore makes sense that we think about what happens when it does. We might also think about any other ways in which the practice of theatre – be it as participant or spectator – might produce distinctive ways of thinking about ethics. It may also make sense to imagine that this might cut both ways and that some consideration of ethics might enable distinctive ways of thinking about (and doing) theatre. This book offers some preliminary thoughts about both. In continuing to sketch out an answer to the question of what is at stake in the bringing together of theatre and ethics, I now outline the shape of the book as a whole.

This book is divided into three chronological parts: 'Ancient', 'Modern' and 'Postmodern'. In this first part, 'Ancient', I consider the legacy of ancient Greek theatre and philosophy and how that legacy might guide us in thinking historically about the relationship between theatre and ethics. Just like theatre and philosophy today, the theatre and philosophy of the ancient Greeks concerned themselves with ethical and political issues, as well as with the relationships between these real-life activities and the fictions about them we create within the field we now call 'art'. In all three parts I explore these relationships and how the practice of theatre both reflects and contributes to the development of social, economic and political relations between the people who make and watch performance. I argue throughout that the ethical dimensions of theatrical production and spectatorship cannot be separated from the specific historical circumstances in which they take place.

Much of this first part addresses the philosophical challenge raised by Plato, whose writing appears to insist that there is something unethical about theatre itself. This idea that theatre itself might be unethical is one to which I return at the end of the book, with the suggestion that an unethical or anti-ethical theatre might be something we both desire and need. It is therefore part of the argument of this book that there is nothing natural, inevitable or even desirable about the conjunction between theatre and ethics suggested by the '&' of my title.

In the second part, 'Modern', I take a huge leap forward in time to examine the origins – social, political, philosophical and theatrical – of the ethical frameworks with which most people in the modern Western world are most familiar. These are the ethical frameworks that take shape when individuals and the societies they form are no longer subjugated to ethical codes imposed from outside or above: by kings or gods. In this modern period the theatre participates in a process of managing the way people think about their relationships with one another and their potential for creating societies in which everyone can enjoy freedom as well as social solidarity. The plays of William Shakespeare offer an early example of the theatre playing this kind of role. Towards the end of the modern period (and the end of the second part of this book) the plays of Bertolt Brecht represent a critical response to this modern ethical framework, and one which ushers in a phase of ethical thought and performance for which I am using the term 'Postmodern' as the title of the third and final part of the book.

In Part Three, I consider the ethical philosophy of Emmanuel Levinas (1906–95), which arose in response to what Levinas (and others) viewed as the disastrous consequences of certain aspects of modern rationality. In this view the genocide committed by the Nazis in the 1940s represented the logical extension of a kind of rationality that had turned both irrational and unethical. Levinasian ethics seeks to replace an ethics based on the freedom of the individual (modern) or the realisation of individual potential (ancient) with an ethics oriented entirely towards the other. Performance conceived in relation to Levinas' postmodern ethics encourages the spectator to stop seeing the performance as an exploration of his or her own subjectivity and, instead, to take it as an opportunity to experience an encounter with someone else. Performance, in this view, invites the spectator to assume ethical responsibility for the fragile life of the other. Here I consider work by the performance group Goat Island and the artist Walid Raad, as well as some recent critical writing about performance.

At the beginning of the twenty-first century, thought about the relationship between theatre and ethics has produced some valuable critical work, upon which I draw in the final part. In such work theatre and performance is valued for, among other things, its own ethical stance and the ethical responses it elicits from spectators. As I suggest in the conclusion to this book, this state of affairs runs the risk of creating a theatrical culture in which performances are valued only for what they might offer in terms of ethics. I therefore end the book with a suggestion that there might also be ethical value in theatre and performance that turns its face away from ethics altogether. But before doing away with ethics, let us find out what it is.

What is ethics?

The word 'ethics' derives from the Greek *ethos* ('character'). We might therefore think of ethics as the study of character. It is not about studying character in a psychological sense, however, as we might when studying a role in a play or a patient in the therapist's room. Ethics as the study of character is not much interested in psychology: it cares little what anyone might feel about his mother, what traumatic events in the past might have shaped someone's behaviour in the present, or what cures might make someone's painful emotional life more bearable. Ethics is interested in character in the sense that it is used when we speak of 'character witnesses'. A character witness is called upon when someone is accused of a crime and wants the court to take into consideration, as evidence in the case, how she normally behaves. The idea is that a character witness will present such a glowing portrait of virtuous and unselfish behaviour that the judge or jury will be convinced that she simply could not have committed the hideous crime of which she has been accused: 'She just doesn't do that sort of thing.' To have committed the crime would have been to 'act out of character'. So, in a certain sense, ethics is about who you really are, deep down. Are you good or bad? Greedy or altruistic? Heroic or cowardly? Psychology might be interested in working out what made you that way. Ethics is not. Ethics is about the kind of person you are.

It is also, of course, about the things that you do. As Beatrice-Joanna in Thomas Middleton and William Rowley's play *The Changeling* (Phoenix Theatre, London, 1622) finds out to her horror once she has commissioned the murder of her husband, she becomes 'the deed's creature' (3.4.137). She may not previously have thought herself the kind of woman who would organise a murder. But the moment she commits such an act, that act becomes part of what makes her who she is. She is created by her own actions: 'the deed's creature'. Part of Neoptolemus' confusion, when he asks himself, 'How shall I act?', arises because he has just done something – lied to Philoctetes – which he had previously thought to be the sort of thing he just did not do. His sense of who he is has been undermined. He is not quite the man he thought he was. We might think of ethics, then, as the thought and practice of acting in keeping with who we think we are. Ethics is about acting in character. There are things we do and things we don't do, and if we wish to think of ourselves in positive terms, from an ethical point of view, the things we do are good, and the things we don't do are not. Ethics is about being good and staying good by acting well.

This sounds quite straightforward on the face of it, but you will already have noticed that there is a problem. How do we know what is good? This question introduces another way of thinking about what ethics might be. We might think of ethics as that branch of human thought concerned with finding out what is good and what is not. We might further imagine that it is the branch of thought that investigates how it might be possible even to know the difference between what is good and what is not. So it is not simply a matter of defining good and evil, of drawing up a set of rules by which to live. It involves working out on what basis, if any, we can make such judgements. On what do we found our conceptions of right and wrong? As I have already suggested, briefly, above, there are certain historical situations in which this kind of question tends to arise more urgently than at other times. Where there is an extremely powerful social consensus around a particular set of rules – as where everyone adheres to the same religion and where that religion, as many do, has definitive texts which prescribe how people should behave – ethics has little work to do. We know what is right and wrong because we have read or heard the sacred texts. It is where this level of unanimity does not exist that the task of ethics becomes demanding.

It is just such a space of ethical uncertainty into which Sophocles inserts Neoptolemus. Ought he simply to do as he is told – obey his elders and respect what appears to be the will of the Gods – or should he strike out on his own and act in accordance with some other set of principles, and if so, which? And where would they come from? Can he just make them up himself? It is in the situation of doubt, in the moment of choice, when you ask yourself, 'How shall I act?', that you are opening up the space of ethics. In posing the question 'How shall I act?' you are also, implicitly, posing a far wider question: 'How can I establish a basis on which to act?' Or, to frame it less personally, 'Can we create a system according to which we will all know how to act?' With that question comes a host of others, such as 'Can we create a system that everyone will agree with?', 'Can we create a system which is entirely rational?', 'How do we balance the claims of individual freedom with those of collective justice?'

Before long these questions, which start out as questions about yourself and an isolated situation in which you don't know what to do, start to become philosophical, and even political. Questions of ethics are involved in how we organise the ways in which we live with one another. Our behaviour never takes place in a vacuum, and our actions always have consequences for people other than ourselves. One of the constant tasks of ethical thought is to assist us in making social and political arrangements that minimise the negative consequences of one individual's actions for the rest of society and also, perhaps, maximise their positive impacts. As we shall see towards the end of this book, much contemporary ethical thought is specifically directed to such questions, including not only our direct, interpersonal relationships with others but the framework within which we conduct relationships with 'others' as such. We began with ethics as the study of character – a definition that might suggest that ethics is all about yourself – but we have ended this brief attempt at a definition with the thought that ethics might in fact be all about everyone but yourself.

Why theatre?

The prime theatrical example I have called on so far – of Neoptolemus' moment of ethical confusion in Sophocles' *Philoctetes* – suggests at least one reason for thinking about theatre and ethics together. Theatre dramatises ethical situations. Furthermore, it does so in specific historical situations. By this I mean the historical situations from which the theatre in question itself emerges. We can reasonably assume that the kind of ethical problems confronting a character in a play, for example, are the sort of things that count as ethical problems in the society in which the play itself was produced. Presumably the dilemmas faced by men involved in war would have been considered significant by Sophocles and his audience in Athens, a state which engaged in successive wars with Persia and Sparta during Sophocles' lifetime, wars in which Sophocles himself participated alongside the fellow citizens who made up the Athenian theatre audience. This indicates a second important factor in how we think theatre and ethics together. Generally speaking, theatre is a social art form. It tends to represent people in social relationships with one another, rather than in isolation. Although it might be possible to imagine a play in which there is no social interaction at all, yet in which an ethical problem is somehow aired, this is not the usual pattern. This means that, in the theatre, ethical problems tend to get presented as social problems, a fact which gives their treatment additional historical specificity. Although, from the great distance of nearly two and a half millennia, the issues confronting Neoptolemus in Sophocles' play can be made to appear somewhat abstract (the account offered above is necessarily schematic), they are unlikely to have been experienced in that way by the audience to whom the play was initially presented. They are far more likely to have been understood in relation to the fabric of the life which the audience and the playwright shared. Similarly, to take a playwright often thought of as a latter-day Sophocles, Henrik Ibsen's *A Doll's House* (Det Kongelige Teater, Copenhagen, 1879) and *Hedda Gabler* (Residenz Theater, Munich, 1891) present not abstract reflections on marriage, childbirth and the life of women but concrete embodiments of a crisis intrinsic to the society about which the plays were written, and in which they were received.

It may be objected that none of this is specific to the theatrical presentation of ethical problems. The same might be said of novels, for example, or of films, both of which present characters in concrete social situations and play out ethical questions through the representation of social action or behaviour. However, theatre makes ethics a social affair in at least one way which is not really available to the novelist or the filmmaker: the dramatisation and social situating of an ethical problem takes place in the presence of the spectator. I wrote this book because I think there is something particular about theatrical spectatorship that offers ways of thinking about ethics – and, specifically, thinking socially and politically about ethics – that no other cultural practice seems to offer. Theatre inserts its ethical questions into the lives of its spectators in a situation in which those spectators are unusually conscious of their own status as spectators, and thus as people who may exercise ethical judgement. It also takes place in the presence of spectators who are aware of their status as spectators who are engaged in reciprocal spectatorship. We watch ourselves watching people engaging with an ethical problem while knowing that we are being watched in our watching (by other spectators and also by those we watch). Because so much ethics is concerned with questions such as the relationship between how people seem and how they are, this situation of mutual spectatorship raises the ethical stakes in theatre in a way that is not quite possible anywhere else. This situation is further complicated by the fact that we tend to know, in the theatre, when people are pretending and when they are not. That is to say, the theatre is a place where we know that there is a difference between how people seem and how they are, but it is also a place where we pretend not to know this difference. It is therefore, perhaps supremely, a place of ethical confusion or cross-purposes. Indeed, if ethics has anything to do with truth – and it is hard to imagine an ethics that has not – then the theatre might be a very strange place to come looking for it. It is, after all, the home of pretending. All the same, people do come to the theatre looking for truth. Perhaps it is the uncertainty about truth and untruth, which is foregrounded in the experience of theatre, that makes it an appealing place to come in search of ethical questions.

The idea that the theatre might be a strange or even inappropriate place to come looking for truth needs to be addressed a little more fully. Here might be the place, then, to consider briefly the idea that the theatre itself should be avoided by anyone interested in his or her own ethical well-being. This is the famous idea that there is something wrong with the theatre, and that the wrong in question is a question of ethics.

What is 'wrong' with theatre?

This famous idea is generally understood to have its most significant point of origin in the work of the Athenian philosopher Plato. Across a range of philosophical works, all written in the form of dialogues, but most famously in *The Republic* (*c*.360 BCE), Plato investigates the nature and consequences of artistic production. He does so within the wider framework of a systematic enquiry into ethics. His most anguished and extensive reflections concern poetry, and, most particularly, those forms of poetry which may be read aloud or performed. It is clear that the practice of reading epic or non-dramatic poetry, such as the works of Homer, formed an important part of public and private life in Plato's Athens. However, it is theatre, and most particularly the tragic theatre of Plato's time, that becomes, in *The Republic*, the art to which his thoughts turn time and again. This has the effect of making theatre itself the paradigm for art in general and the location for the development of important elements in Plato's ethical thought. The ultimate test for theatre is to what extent it can make a positive contribution to the development of the human individual towards self-fulfilment or self-realisation. For Plato, the highest aim of a human being should be to achieve the life of the philosopher, engaged in the pursuit and contemplation of truth. Encouraging this aim is the basis of his ethics. If theatre can support such an aim, then it has a place in the imaginary ideal world of *The Republic*. But if it cannot make such a contribution, it has no place there.

For Plato, the highest achievement of the human is reason. Imagination, in contrast, is entangled with emotions. The task of reason is to keep emotion in check, so as to maintain the coherence and stability of the individual human being. If theatre overwhelms its spectators with their own emotions and encourages them to imagine that human identity might be unstable or changeable, then theatre will have to be resisted. This tension between reason and emotion, or between rational thought and the imagination, has recurred in ethical thought, about theatre and about life in general, from Plato's day to our own.

The dialogue form in which Plato writes (with his lead character, Socrates, in constant conversation with other characters who seek his wisdom) already points to a spirit of contradiction in those works where both dramatic representation and poetry are subjected to systematic critique. As many critics have noted, Plato's attack on poetry and on tragic theatre in particular is launched from within poetry itself. His rationalism is presented by way of a work of the imagination. In *The Republic* Socrates acknowledges that 'even the best of us enjoy it [poetry] and let ourselves be carried away by our feelings; and we are full of praises for the merits of the poet who can most powerfully affect us in this way' (p. 349). In his concluding remarks on the subject in Book Ten of *The Republic*, Socrates acknowledges that persuasive arguments might be made on behalf of poetry and its ethical value. However, he warns, 'If they fail to make their case, then we shall have to follow the example of the lover who renounces a passion that is doing him no good, however hard it may be to do so' (p. 351). Later, Plato's student Aristotle, in his *Poetics* (*c*.330 BCE), will seek to advance persuasive arguments in favour of poetry (including theatre), proposing that theatre can be good for both the individual and society, as it encourages the training of the emotions away from excess and towards moderation. Aristotle's arguments have been much more enthusiastically received by supporters of the theatre than Plato's. That is itself a good reason for paying close attention to Plato's views.

The charges laid by Plato at theatre's door are various. Poets do not know what they are talking about. Although Homer writes of war, he never commanded an army in battle, never devised any technology that might enhance an army's capacity to fight, and never founded a school of any kind to pass on his knowledge. Instead, Homer, and all the poets who have followed him, merely produce superficial representations of the world, including representations of human capacity. Their work is based on what things look like rather than how they truly are. For Plato, for whom actual objects in the world are only second-order representations of their 'ideal form', the productions of poets and artists are therefore copies twice removed from reality itself.

In inviting audiences to take these copies for real, theatre not only leads them into a confusion about reality, with all the ethical problems that a failure to distinguish truth from fiction must entail; it also encourages them to prioritise emotion over reason. This is because the moment you start reciting poetry or performing a role in a play, you are, according to Plato, sucked into inhabiting the psychology, emotions and ethical position of the character you are representing. Thus the whole and integrated self, which is supposed to be held together by reason, is made fluid and transformable by accessing feelings and emotions that are not really its own. Imagination put into action by performance might lead you to imagine what it could be like to be someone else or to desire a different kind of life from that which is available. By instilling such false ideas of potential transformation, theatre undermines your capacity to be happy in the life that you are actually living.

In Book Three of *The Republic*, this dangerous self-transformation is the risk associated with performing, and this contributes to an argument that performance should not form part of the education of a full citizen but should be undertaken only by people, such as slaves, whose human development and self-realisation is not an issue for Plato. Here the enjoyment by an audience of performance (including music, poetry and their combination in the theatre) is not the real problem. However, in Book Ten the threat of self-dissolution through the encounter with performed emotion extends to the audience. As Stephen Halliwell writes in *The Aesthetics of Mimesis* (2002), 'What was there the performer's "self-likening" now seems to have become the emotional assimilation of the entire theater audience' (p. 78). Everyone, then, is caught up in a sequence of emotional states which replace the single reasoning self and which produce a systemic failure properly to distinguish between true and false, good and bad. Furthermore, the theatre typically represents people behaving badly (killing the king, sleeping with mother). With an audience divested of its reason and its capacity to tell good from bad, there is thus an acute danger that people will be corrupted by the desire to emulate the bad behaviour of the characters they see represented on stage. This, for Plato, is the most serious objection to poetry: 'It has a terrible power to corrupt even the best characters, with very few exceptions' (*The Republic*, p. 349). It is certainly no use at all as a source of ethical teaching. This is precisely Plato's point and the problem at issue for him: in the Athens of his day it was a commonplace assumption that the poets, and their latest achievement, the tragic theatre, constituted a worthwhile source of philosophical understanding and moral guidance. The vehemence with which Plato seems to condemn the theatre is partly due to the disproportionate ethical value assigned to theatre by his contemporaries.

Plato does not seem, then, to be a very productive site on which to try to construct a positive account of theatre's relation to ethics: the poets are to be expelled from the Republic and the theatres closed. However, Plato's thought does raise further and more complex problems for theatre and for any consideration of its relation to ethics. These problems are perhaps best approached by rethinking some of Plato's objections to theatre and poetry.

One might argue, first, that the issue of artistic representation is in fact more complex than this account of Plato suggests. What if Plato's critique is aimed not so much at the production of images and representations as at the way in which they are received? Such images are only 'false' if they are erroneously taken to be what they represent. If they are understood, from the outset, to be representations, then no one is fooled. The issue of their value lies not in the extent to which they represent accurately the superficial appearance of that which they represent but in what meaning or sense might be made by the viewer or spectator in the act of reception. The value of a painting does not lie in the extent to which it looks like the real thing but elsewhere, in the thought (about the world, about representation) to which it gives rise. Plato's critique here, which uses painting as its example, may be directed not at painting (or representation) in general but at certain kinds of painting (or representation) that merely seek to achieve superficial likeness and no more, and at viewers who see no more than a pretty picture that looks like the landscape it depicts.

Second, and in the specific instance of the theatre, Plato seems to be laying the grounds for an argument that a theatre which appeals to the emotions alone – to sympathy and identification, for example – lacks ethical value. Perhaps it is not sufficient to build ethics on sympathy. One may sympathise or identify with someone without having to approve of his or her actions. The basis of an ethical relationship with others surely depends on a suspension of self-interest. An ethics based solely on the capacity to sympathise would be a hollow ethics, founded on nothing but the kind of fellow-feeling that could readily tip over into xenophobia. Plato is warning against a theatre that enlists our sympathy for people like us and that, in doing so, threatens to turn our hostility towards people who are not like us. An ethical theatre would encourage us to fight our own prejudices, all too readily expressed in our emotions, and to see the potential good in those we have until now been taught to think of as the 'bad' other. Of course, much theatre has sought to achieve just this reversal, precisely by seeking to excite sympathy for the other. A famous early example of this is Aeschylus' *The Persians* (Athens, 472 BCE), in which an Athenian audience is clearly encouraged to feel strong sympathy for the defeated enemy of the Athenian state. For Plato, though, as perhaps also for Brecht in the twentieth century, distance rather than identification is the path to an ethical theatre, and so a reversal of the terms on which identification is made (we cheer for the 'other' or 'bad' guy rather than the 'good' guy) is not enough. The problem is the idea that our ethical judgement should be based on emotional identification.

The third and final development of Plato's thought concerns tragic theatre in particular, which, as Stephen

Halliwell argues, is not merely a theatrical form but presents a distinctive, tragic, view of the world. Halliwell contends that Plato preceded philosophers of the tragic in identifying the tragic as a kind of philosophy, or view of the world. For most of the later thinkers, the tragic is something to be embraced, in a sober or deeply pessimistic reckoning with the harshness of human existence. For Plato, the tragic is to be resisted as something 'fundamentally hostile to human needs and values and irreconcilable with a positive moral significance' (p. 109). The tragic worldview, as encountered by Plato in the poems and dramas of his own age, proposes that the world is irredeemably entangled with evil for which the Gods themselves bear responsibility, that death is an evil to be feared, that the death of those you love is final and irrecuperable, and that there is no necessary correlation between justice and happiness: the good are punished and the evil get away with it. If the best human life is the life of the philosopher, ruled by reason, contemplating and seeking out truth, this kind of theatre, which presents what is, for Plato, a wholly untrue picture of human existence, represents a barrier to attaining such a life. In *The Fragility of Goodness* (1986) Martha Nussbaum takes this idea a stage further in her suggestion that in his philosophical dialogues Plato is seeking not merely to repudiate this tragic philosophy but to replace it, both philosophically and theatrically. The dialogues, suggests Nussbaum, model a new post-tragic theatre, 'constructed to supplant tragedy as the paradigm of ethical teaching' (p. 129). Tragedy is the theatre and philosophy of a political and religious order which Plato seeks to overturn. It peddles dangerously pessimistic illusions that encourage a fearful audience to submit to inexorable fate rather than struggle to imagine the world differently. 'By writing philosophy as drama,' Nussbaum continues, 'Plato calls on every reader to engage actively in the search for truth' (p. 134) rather than comply, albeit ecstatically, with the old lies.

Such a view of Plato might be encouraged by a properly historical consideration of his work. We might think of Plato as a thinker engaged in a struggle with other philosophers, such as his contemporaries, the Sophists, whose appeal was based on talking well and plausibly rather than on truth. We might also see him struggling against a social consensus in which old religion discouraged new thought. We might thus reveal Plato not as an anti-theatrical thinker at all but as a thinker of theatre who demands more and better from the theatre than dramatic illusionism, one who seeks a theatre which acknowledges distance and creates productive opportunities for the spectator, and one who, crucially, offers substantive encouragement to a thinking of theatre in relation to ethics. Plato argued against a specific form of theatre, against a particular philosophical position which it embodied, and not, after all, against theatre itself. Plato turns out to be one of the most significant theorists of the relationship between theatre and ethics, demanding that theatre ought to justify itself in terms of the contribution it might make to an ethical life.

Part Two

modern

'How shall I act?' When Neoptolemus asked this question he may have hoped to receive an answer from someone or somewhere else. Ethics in its modern period begins from the assumption that there is no someone or somewhere else to provide such an answer. Neoptolemus might have hoped for a god, or even just an authoritative leader, to guide him in what to do. In pre-modern periods of European history ethical philosophy held that certain fundamental principles could be attributed to divine sources (in most of Europe, the Christian god). Shared concepts of good and evil were sustained by religious and political institutions and enforced as social norms. Although it might have been the responsibility of each individual to consider her actions in ethical terms – to ask herself how to act – she had a commonly agreed framework against which to measure choices and determine ethical value. In effect, the individual was supposed to observe universal laws and had no autonomy: she could not make her own ethics. When and why did this framework start to break down, and what did ethical theory have to offer to replace it? The first sections of Part Two trace the process by which modern Europe invented autonomy, during a period spanning the sixteenth to the eighteenth century.

Two key terms deserve a brief exposition here: 'modernity' and 'enlightenment'. Both, of course, are complex and contested. For the purposes of the argument that follows, though, take 'modernity' to refer to a set of social and economic circumstances that came to their fullest fruition from the middle of the nineteenth century in Europe (explained in more detail in the first section below), and take 'enlightenment' to refer to a set of philosophical and scientific developments that established reason as the supreme principle of human life and that sought to be the master-narrative of modernity itself (explored more fully in the second section below). These interlinked processes – social, economic and philosophical – may be understood as the complex foundations for the emergence of the autonomous individual who would, from then on, be solely responsible for making her own ethical decisions. We may also call this autonomous individual the bourgeois subject, for the individual making ethical choices is an individual in a particular social and historical situation, one in which power is gradually moving away from kings and queens who seem to derive their authority from God towards merchants and industrialists whose power, as we shall see, is founded on economic success in a capitalist society.

Modernity and the bourgeois subject

Modernity involved a rapidly developing capitalist economy, driven by constant technological innovation in modes of production, communication and transport. In concrete terms it is often regarded as the period of the rise of the city as the dominant political and social force in Europe, the period of railway travel, electricity, mass production, the department store and, eventually, the cinema, aeroplanes, telephones and world war. It is also a period widely associated with the total dissolution and reformulation of traditional social relationships and religious and moral values. In the words of Karl Marx and Friedrich Engels, in their *Communist Manifesto* (1848), it is what happens when 'all that is solid melts into air' (p. 223).

Working out when this process begins and when we start being modern is a tricky business, and one that tends to depend on what you think being modern means. The widespread use in literary (and theatrical) studies of the term 'early modern' to define the period when Shakespeare wrote and acted in his plays suggests that the critics using this term have identified in the culture of that time something that will grow up to be characteristically modern. They might, for example, claim to see in the culture of late sixteenth- and early seventeenth-century London a precursor of the urban life that was to become the defining social feature of full-blown nineteenth-century modernity. They might also discern within that culture the emergence of new ways of thinking about human subjectivity and relationships between human subjects. In the London of this time they might observe the emergence of new kinds of powerful people (usually men) who acquired their political power and social prestige by means of economic success. These were individuals whose authority was actively acquired rather than given to them as the consequence of aristocratic family lineage. Just as they acquired power and wealth through the use of their own wits and energies, so they framed their subjectivities, and thus their ethics: the 'self-made man' is not one to subject himself to laws made for him by others. In comic plays of city life by writers such as Ben Jonson, energetic young men from modest backgrounds use the gift of the gab and the tricks of the trade to make good in the marketplaces of London. They use their skills of pretence and simulation to practise confidence tricks on the slow-witted aristocracy, often aiming at that ultimate prize of bedding and wedding the daughter. These men are the bourgeois subject in the making.

The plays communicate an acute ambivalence about such figures. On the one hand, these characters are often the source of the narrative and theatrical energy of the plays. They are where the action is; they talk to the audience; they have the best jokes and the cleverest moves. But the plays in question have a tendency to close with their defeat. In Jonson's *The Alchemist* (Blackfriars, London, 1610), for example, the deceptions of the fake gold-producer, Face, are precisely what produce the audience's pleasure in the play. These deceptions are also, explicitly, about the successful manipulation of a new kind of economy, in which the entrepreneur and the con artist are two sides of the same coin. Face is the embodiment of this duplicitous double figure, and though his performance is fundamental to the vitality of the play, his defeat is structurally necessary. The play reaffirms the legitimacy of the old economic order by exposing Face's deceptions, having already exposed the frailty of that very same old order through its theatrical celebration of the energies of the new.

Shakespeare's *King Lear* (Whitehall, London, 1606) offers a much more overtly political vision of what happens in the transition between a hierarchical society ruled by a monarch and a new social formation in which there is a struggle for power between contending forces. The play is about the shift not just from one generation to another (father to son, father to daughter) but from one social order to another (put very simply, from feudalism to capitalism). After a long scene in which an aging monarch makes an appalling mess of his succession, a young man takes the stage and addresses the audience:

> Thou, Nature, art my goddess; to thy law
> My services are bound. Wherefore should I
> Stand in the plague of custom, and permit
> The curiosity of nations to deprive me?
> For that I am some twelve or fourteen moonshines
> Lag of a brother? Why bastard? Wherefore base?
> When my dimensions are as well compact,
> My mind as generous and my shape as true
> As honest madam's issue? (1.2.1–9)

Edmund, bastard son of the Earl of Gloucester, sets out his challenge to the established order. He will act according to his own nature. He repudiates those laws that say he is illegitimate, and he refuses to suffer because 'nations' invent strange hierarchies according to which he is judged inferior. He is as good a man as any other, including his legitimate brother. This is so because of his intrinsic worth (his dimensions, his mind and his shape) rather than because of anything God or his parents have given him. Edmund here makes explicit at the philosophical level what is implied in the activities of the self-made men of the city comedies. He articulates his desire for precisely what Alasdair MacIntyre, in *After Virtue* (1985), asserts that the moral philosophy of the enlightenment and modernity claimed to have achieved: 'The self had been liberated from all those outmoded forms of social organisation which had imprisoned it simultaneously within a belief in a theistic and teleological world order and within those hierarchical structures which attempted to legitimate themselves as part of such a world order' (p. 58).

As plays such as *The Alchemist* and *King Lear* represent, social and economic developments in the 'early modern' period have started to throw up modes of being and thinking that challenge the ethical frameworks that both sustain and are sustained by the existing social and political order. The people doing this being and thinking have to produce a new ethical framework, one by which they might be able to live the good life and which might legitimate their own economic and social power rather than confirm or consolidate the power of the old order. Edmund's way – the complete absence of any ethics at all – looks disastrous. If human beings simply act according to their 'Nature', then two ruinous consequences follow. First, life will be a vicious battle for power, wealth and self-gratification in which every man (and woman) is in it for him (or herself). Second, this state of social anarchy will draw down upon it the fiercest form of absolutist tyranny. Faced with this rather gloomy prospect, ethical theory took up the task of finding some kind of middle way between 'Do as you are told' and 'Do as you please'. Or, to put it another way, philosophers started to grapple with the competing claims of autonomy and universality, and, in particular, to see whether they could find a reasonable basis for an ethical framework that achieved universality on the one hand, without compromising the freedom of the autonomous individual (the bourgeois subject) on the other. This attempt to construct such an ethical framework is one way of defining the enlightenment project. The next section considers how this project entered the theatres of eighteenth-century Europe.

Enlightenment and the theatre as ethical institution

The enlightenment is sometimes represented as something that was going on in the minds of philosophers and simply overlapped with the beginning of modernity. It refers most frequently to philosophical and scientific projects in the mid- to late eighteenth century in which the powers of human reason triumph over a range of forces of darkness: superstition, ignorance and arbitrary political power. Its projects range widely, from the compilation in France of an encyclopaedia in which the state of human knowledge can be summarised and made available to all to the development of new philosophical work in the field of ethics, most notably in Germany, France and Scotland. The emphasis throughout, though, is on the capacity of human reason to provide solutions both to problems of knowledge and understanding and to material problems, such as how to build bridges. Reason is not simply a process of thinking about the world and how it works; it becomes a means for shaping and controlling the world and how it works. Thus, enlightenment and modernity are entangled in one another, as the challenges of new economic situations call forth rational solutions from the minds of philosophers and engineers alike. Part and parcel of modernity, then, is the pervasive belief that the world can be controlled by the power of human reason. Enlightenment philosophy may be understood, at least in part, as an attempt to construct an ethics that will legitimate the bourgeois subject and the social and economic power it has obtained through the exercise of its reason.

Reason alone was not enough, though, for the philosophers of the enlightenment. The natural faculty of human emotion was also accorded a central role in the development of ethical theory at this time. Reason could function for Plato as a superior form of mental activity which could control such lower and potentially unruly functions as the emotions. For Plato reason was the ally of ethical conduct because it prevented feelings from taking control of the body and leading the human subject into all kinds of naughtiness. For many thinkers of the enlightenment, however, human feeling could not so easily be dismissed or subjected to control. As the human subject came to be understood as the key figure in the enlightenment universe – eventually, for many, displacing God from this position – it made sense to think of the human subject as the origin of goodness. Human feelings, as the spontaneous responses to the experience of the world, might themselves be ethical or could at least be understood as the basis for an innate or natural goodness upon which humans could base their ethical conduct and theory.

Adam Smith (1723–90) was a Scottish enlightenment philosopher, more famous as the author of one of the founding texts of economic liberalism (*The Wealth of Nations*, 1776) than as an ethical philosopher. In 1759 he published a significant contribution to ethical thought, *The Theory of Moral Sentiments*, in which feeling plays a prominent part. The book's particular significance in our context is that it proposes a theatrical way of thinking about ethics, in which we judge our own behaviour in the guise of an imaginary 'spectator' within us. As his title suggests, Smith's ethical thought is founded in an understanding of human emotion. It is 'sentimentalist' in a specific philosophical sense. This does not mean that Smith was in the habit of bursting into tears when presented with cards with pictures of cute kittens on them but rather that he based his understanding of human behaviour on a theory of 'sentiments', or feelings. For sentimentalists, ethical judgements derive from sentiments, or expressions of a special kind of emotion which comes about from the disinterested observation of the behaviour of other people. When we approve of someone's action, we experience this approval as pleasure, and when we disapprove of what someone does, we experience displeasure or anxiety. We experience these feelings as a result of the operations of what Smith and other philosophers of the time called 'sympathy'.

Like 'sentimental', 'sympathy' had a precise meaning at the time. It was understood as a form of physiological communication between human beings. Given that all human beings share more or less the same organic features and, with these, more or less the same sensations and emotions, the 'idea' of what someone else is feeling or doing can impose itself upon my own human organism as an 'impression'. In the process of an 'impression', something happens to me as a physiological being. As the term itself suggests, it is 'impressed' upon me; it is like the action of a printing press on the surface of a body. As a result of this process of 'impression' I experience the feeling along with the other person. Literally, I feel the same thing. The operation is not just the communication of an 'idea', which would be merely intellectual, but the communication of a passion, from one body to another. The operation of sympathy, by which we feel as others feel, is what enables us to experience pleasure in our approval of what others do when they do good, and to feel displeasure or even pain when they do wrong. Human beings thus possess, in their interactions with one another, a capacity for ethical judgement which is a natural extension of their existence as physiological beings. For Adam Smith this understanding of human interaction opened the way for the development of an ethical theory based on theatrical spectatorship. In short, each of us carries within us an 'impartial spectator', to whom we refer our own actions for ethical judgement. If we sense that our impartial spectator approves of our actions, we may judge our actions to be good and right. We have to be able to sympathise with ourselves in the act of imagining ourselves to be spectators of our own action.

But this capacity for sympathy is not simply about feeling sorry for someone. It is an emotion which carries within it an element of disinterest. The kind of spectatorship that Smith is using as his model is one in which individuals, in making ethical judgements, must separate themselves into two subjectivities – the one who judges and the one whose action is judged. This distance – the distance marked out by the act of sympathising with oneself – is what distinguishes this kind of ethical judgement from simply doing as you please or acting in whatever way makes you feel good. For Tracy Davis, in 'Theatricality and Civil Society' (2004), this is what is meant by 'theatricality': 'it is the act of withholding sympathy that makes us become spectators to ourselves and others' (p. 154). A doubling of the self in which both reason and emotion are at work, in which there is an attempt to measure one against the other and let neither obliterate the other, becomes the basis for an ethical position. As Davis points out, in the twentieth century this will become for Brecht, above all, the basis for a critical theatrical practice. Brecht's 'theatricality' is often presented as though it sought to remove emotion altogether. This consideration of his eighteenth-century theoretical predecessor, Adam Smith, reveals that the process of distantiation depends upon holding both reason and emotion in play at the same time. Davis, like Smith and Brecht, argues for the positive value of 'active dissociation, or alienation, or self-reflexivity in standing aside from the suffering of the righteous to name and thus bring into being the self-possession of a critical stance' (p. 153). It is obvious that reason is required to perform this act of 'active dissociation'. Less obvious, but just as vital, is the role of emotion in identifying and sympathising with the suffering in the first place, thus creating the object from which the critical stance of ethics can stand aside.

'How shall I act?' Perhaps the most famous and influential 'modern' answer to this question comes from Immanuel Kant (1724–1804) in his *Groundwork for the Metaphysics of Morals* (1785): 'Act in accordance with that maxim which can at the same time make itself into a universal law' (p. 55). To act ethically one must consider what would happen if one's action – reading someone's private diary, for example – could reasonably be turned into a rule that everyone should follow. Only if one can reasonably imagine an action being adopted as a rule for everyone can it be considered ethically good. This is another way of expressing the idea considered in Part One that ethics might be based on treating all other people as ends rather than as means. To treat someone as a means of achieving some personal goal is not a course of action that one can logically propose that everyone should follow. If it were established as a universal law, everyone would simply be competing to assert her own will at the expense of the desires of others. It would involve the subjection of one's own freedom and desires to the desires of others, while simultaneously subjecting the desires of the others to one's own desires.

This is often called the 'categorical imperative'. The ethics derived from this principle is a way of regulating the actions of the individual by way of the needs of the collective, or of managing the relationship between the particular (individual) and the universal (humanity at large). Another way of phrasing this 'universal' principle would be to propose that everyone should act autonomously so as, simultaneously, to preserve the autonomy of everyone else. The autonomous individual – one who gives herself her own law – would have to be able to produce, for herself, an ethical law that would also be applicable to everyone else, bearing in mind that 'everyone else' comprises a collection of other autonomous individuals, who cannot, by definition, accept a law from anyone other than themselves. Thus Kant's categorical imperative is an attempt to reconcile the autonomy of the individual with the requirement that ethics be universal. It is also, therefore, an attempt to reconcile the purely rational with the empirical, or, in other words, to bring thought and feeling together. It proposes, in short, that there exists within each of us a specifically human capacity to feel what is right. The individual becomes, in effect, a universal subject, capable of producing ethics without referring to any external law, power or god.

This represents one of the great emancipatory achievements of the enlightenment and the bourgeois revolution of which it formed part. In its historical moment it was part of a widespread attempt to derive a set of universal (and broadly progressive) values from the worldview of a rational bourgeois subject. One means by which these values could be explored and affirmed would be the theatre, a place where the individual subject (or central character of a drama) might become, in the eyes of the public, a universal figure or subject. It was in the Germany of the eighteenth century that one of the most significant attempts to make theatre an ethical and civic institution took place. Germany did not, at this time, exist as a unified nation; instead, it comprised a set of interrelated cultural, linguistic and political societies, with no one city establishing itself as a cultural centre (as London and Paris had already done). The enlightenment in Germany therefore often saw itself as part of a project of national identity formation. Rational government would gradually abolish all the minor states, ruled by aristocrats, and replace them with a modern nation. German scholarship on classical (Greek) civilisation provided a powerful ideological model for what this modern nation might be. The idea that the theatre might be an ethical institution, capable of encouraging the development of ethical modern citizens, clearly owed much to the high esteem in which the élite culture of enlightenment Germany held Greek political and theatrical life. In Germany, therefore, in the absence of an actual nation, an ideological construct took hold in which it became possible to imagine the ethical and political value of a 'national theatre' as a location for the propagation of new enlightenment and bourgeois values, through the creation of a new and distinctly 'national' culture.

A thorough theoretical and practical development of this construct is to be found in the work of the playwright and aesthetic theorist Gotthold Ephraim Lessing (1729–81). Lessing sought to show that the emergent new bourgeois class could be both subject matter and spectators of tragic drama. The purpose of their being both subject matter and spectators was to kindle in bourgeois society a 'modern' community of feeling, similar to the social cohesion that Lessing found articulated in Aristotle's writing on tragic drama in his *Poetics*. When Lessing came to write his own quasi-theoretical work on theatre – in the 104 short essays and reviews that make up his *Hamburg Dramaturgy* (1767–9) – he argued that the fortunes of traditional tragic protagonists no longer aroused the emotions of the theatre audience. In the fourteenth 'dramatic note', written immediately after a performance of his first major play, *Miss Sara Sampson* (Ackermannsche Gesellschaft, Frankfurt an der Oder, 1755), he wrote:

> The names of princes and heroes can lend pomp and majesty to a play, but they contribute nothing to our emotion. The misfortunes of those whose circumstances most resemble our own, must naturally penetrate most deeply into our hearts, and if we pity kings we pity them as human beings, not as kings. (pp. 38–9)

Here Lessing is starting to articulate a distinction between the Aristotelian emotions of 'pity and terror', familiar from his *Poetics*, and a tragic theatre that is to be founded in 'compassion'. Rather than a community united in a common fear produced by witnessing the calamities that befall heroes, Lessing is seeking to produce, through bourgeois tragedy, a public that will learn from the theatre how to feel compassion for their fellow humans. Out of that compassion a genuine nation would be created. A people bound together by compassion for one another, as human beings, would constitute a modern Germany, modelled partly on an imaginary Athens. Lessing wrote dramas designed to create such a theatre. The theatre would be the institution in which citizens of a unified German nation would gather, out of passionate interest rather than idle curiosity, to renew their emotional and ethical commitment to the idea and reality of that nation.

However, there is also a danger inherent in such a project. This newly inclusive theatre, in which the bourgeoisie of the modern nation gather to feel compassion for one another, might easily turn into part of a new kind of exclusive culture that understands its own feelings and values – be they 'German', 'modern', 'civilised', 'European' – as intrinsically better than those from which they differ. Because this theatre presents its values as 'universal' and its culture as something to which the whole of humanity may aspire, it makes the implicit claim that anyone who does not participate in that culture (foreigners, people who do not go to the theatre, for example) is somehow defective. The universal concept of 'human' which this theatre seeks to promote can easily lapse into 'humans like me'. Values which are actually specific to a class and a culture (bourgeois Europeans) come to be felt and understood as universal in ways they might not be. This came to be the basis of much of the twentieth-century critique of enlightenment, as Part Three of this book shows.

Against bourgeois universalism: Bertolt Brecht

Before turning to Part Three, I would like to close Part Two with a brief comment on a play which might usefully be seen as the end-point of a certain trajectory of German ethical drama: Brecht's *Der Gute Mensch von Sezuan* (Schauspielhaus, Zürich, 1943), usually translated as *The Good Person of Szechwan*. The dramas of Lessing and his contemporaries might be seen as earlier phases of this trajectory. Brecht's play brings to a close, I suggest, a model of the big-stage play with a historical or fabulous narrative in which the ethical dilemmas of a central bourgeois figure are deployed to res-onate with the ethico-political concerns of a clearly defined modern public. In bringing that model to a close it also presents a thorough critique of the ethics embodied in such plays. For Brecht all these plays have a politically objection-able tendency to present their particular values – based on the values of a particular class and nation – as though they were universally applicable, even to people with radically different class positions and political desires. Brecht's play is often seen as a satirical comment on the uselessness of ethics in the material context of poverty and political inequality. I want to suggest that if it is this, it is also a commentary on the uselessness of the theatre as a site for 'moral instruction'. This is how it represents the end-point of the dramatic tradition of which it forms part.

Three Gods have been dispatched to Earth with a mission to find at least one good person. If they can do so, it seems, the Earth can be saved. As the play begins, they are already dismayed by what they find. 'Circumstances' are taking their toll on the people of Earth. The water-seller Wang does his best to find lodgings for the Gods for the night, but no one opens his door, until Wang turns, as anyone involved in such a parable might, to the prostitute Shen Te. She makes the Gods welcome in her tiny room, and the following morning they leave convinced that, at last, they have found a good person. They decide to bend the rules of their mission and reward Shen Te by paying for their accommodation. Once they have gone, Shen Te discovers that they have left her a thousand silver dollars. She buys a tobacconist's shop. She is at once besieged by people seeking to take advantage of her good fortune: a huge family moves into the shop, a carpenter and the landlady demand immediate payments for shelving and advance rent, and, worst of all, she falls for Yang Sun, a suicidal young man who dreams of becoming an airman and for whom she is willing to sacrifice everything to help him move to Peking and fly mail planes. To contend with all these demands she creates a no-nonsense male cousin, Shui Ta, in whose persona she intervenes to cheat the carpenter, fend off the needy family, and, gradually, build her modest tobacco store into a thriving business based on the exploitation of everyone else (in some versions of the play this involves the establishment of a neighbourhood heroin business). The situation is complicated further as Shen Te finds herself pregnant. Now Shui Ta must fight even more fiercely in response to Shen Te's love for her child to come. Shen Te disappears and Shui Ta prospers. People in the neighbourhood become suspicious, fearing that the hardnosed businessman has somehow done away with his angelic cousin. Shui Ta is arrested and a trial ensues. Wang the water-seller succeeds in having the Gods replace the judge, in the hope that they will uncover what Shui Ta has done to their one remaining 'good person'. Under the pressure of questioning Shui Ta breaks down and confesses that he is in fact Shen Te. She has been unable to live and be good at the same time. The Gods, delighted to have found their one good person alive after all, make a hasty retreat to Heaven, insisting that they can do nothing to make her life any easier.

This is, of course, a playfully cynical demystification of ethical norms. It sets out to show that a fixed set of ethical values that might add up to such a being as 'the good person' is impossible given the social and economic conditions under which we live. The Gods come across as a trio of bourgeois do-gooders, eager to find and champion their 'Angel of the Slums' but quite unwilling to do anything about the structural inequalities that capitalism imposes upon the people of Szechwan. The desire to be 'good' is presented as a form of deadly addiction, mirrored by Shui Ta's adoption of heroin

as his main business. If Shen Te is initially the main victim of this desire to be good, she is not alone. Bourgeois
do-gooders also enjoy the theatre, particularly, one might
suspect, the theatre that establishes itself as a site for moral
instruction and the acquisition of goodness. Perhaps, then,
we might think of the Gods as the typical bourgeois theatre
audience, and the play – in which they finally escape from
the theatre, never to return – as a sly attack on its own audience's desire to seek out ethical nourishment in the theatre.
As the Gods depart they seem to express their appreciation
of a little world which has tugged at their heartstrings:

> This little world
> Has quite captivated us. Your joys and sorrows
> Have refreshed us and touched us. (p. 239, my
> translation)

It is as though they are a theatre audience who have got
what they came for. They have been 'captivated' by a 'little
world', and in the process their own emotions have been
'refreshed' through an encounter with the suffering of others.
They can go home now, just like the spectators at a tragedy as envisaged by Aristotle, a little emotion safely spent
to make themselves feel better. It is not only the values of
the bourgeois enlightenment that are subject to Brecht's critique here but also the very idea that going to the theatre
might in any way be good for you.

Part Three

postmodern

Brecht stands at a crossroads. His work is readily understood within the terms of enlightenment modernity.
His theatrical practice itself is a process of demystification.
It opposes a form of 'scientific' rationality to the narcotics
of illusionism. His political commitment to Marxism places
his thought and work firmly on the side of progress. So far,
so enlightenment. But his practice is also characterised by
a deliberate courting of uncertainty. In *The Good Person of
Szechwan* nothing is offered by way of an alternative to the
despairing departure of the Gods. The problems remain
problems, and the theatre seems an increasingly unlikely
place to look for solutions. Even in what are frequently
viewed as his most doctrinaire, scientific-socialist hardliner
works, the *Lehrstücke* ('Teaching Plays'), this uncertainty
turns out to be at the core of his practice. Brecht's is at one
and the same time a theatre of enlightenment modernity,
ideologically committed to progress and to the realisation

of universal goals, and a theatre that radically challenges the very structure of enlightenment thought, through an interest in process and openness much more regularly associated with the postmodern.

Teaching ethics

Brecht's *The Decision* (Großes Schauspielhaus, Berlin, 1930) is a play in which four Communist agitators report back on their mission to spread Communist teachings to the people of Mukden. During the course of their mission they are joined by a Young Comrade, a local Communist who acts as their guide. The four agitators set the Young Comrade a series of revolutionary tasks, and on each occasion he fails, because he is unable to separate feeling from reason (precisely what Shen Te tries to achieve in *The Good Person of Szechwan*, through the invention of Shui Ta). Thus the Young Comrade keeps intervening in situations in ways that jeopardise the objectives of the mission. As a result of his final failure, a riot breaks out, forcing the agitators to escape back across the border. They cannot take the Young Comrade with them, nor can they leave him behind (as his presence would betray their mission). They have ten minutes in which to decide what to do. They decide to shoot him and bury him in a lime pit. The Young Comrade agrees that this is the right thing to do. The 'Control Chorus' to whom they report this story, and to whose verdict on their action they have agreed in advance to submit themselves, announces that it agrees with their decision.

On the face of it this looks like a parable designed to teach the virtues of strict adherence to Communist Party discipline. As the Control Chorus announces:

> At the same time your report shows us how much
> Is needed if our world is to be altered:
> Rage and stubbornness, knowledge and rebellion
> Quick reactions, profound meditation
> Icy patience, endless repetition
> Awareness of little things and awareness of big ones:
> Only studying reality
> Helps us alter reality. (p. 89)

The form of the play, though, suggests something rather less straightforward. First, although the *Lehrstücke* were performed in theatres, they were initially experiments in a kind of participatory theatre without public performances. As Brecht himself writes in an essay entitled 'The German Drama: Pre-Hitler' (1936), reprinted in *Brecht on Theatre* (1977), 'These experiments were theatrical performances meant not so much for the spectator as for those who were engaged in the performance. It was, so to speak, art for the producer, not art for the consumer' (p. 80). Even as a performance for an audience, the plays were intended not so much to deliver messages as to provoke discussions. The presentation of a series of actions, in each of which decisions are held up for evaluation by both the 'Control Chorus' and the audience, has the effect of highlighting the moment of decision, the fact that a decision has to be taken. In this way, the capacity for decision-making, the availability of political and ethical options, is foregrounded, in contrast to what Brecht believed happened in what he called 'the aristotelian play', whose 'task', he wrote, was 'to show the world as it is' (p. 79). This effect is enhanced by the specification that the actors playing the four agitators should, as they present their report scenes, rotate through the available roles, so that no single actor is permanently associated with any particular character. Here again the aim seems to be to focus on the mechanics of the situation and the decision rather than on the 'fate' of the Young Comrade. This points towards the second, and perhaps most significant way, in which *The Decision*, and the *Lehrstücke* more generally, were more complex and less didactic than they seem. As Reiner Steinweg has argued in *Das Lehrstück* (1972), these plays were actually intended as the basis for a process of ongoing rehearsal, in which all possible decisions and their consequences could be explored. The text is not a finished text but an open field for a process of improvisation, rewriting and discussion. This, rather than public performance, is how Brecht and his collaborators sought to create a theatre for its producers rather than for an audience of consumers. The practice of theatre becomes a collective labour of political and ethical exploration.

Brecht's *Lehrstücke* clearly act as a precursor to such more recent practices as Augusto Boal's Forum Theatre, in which social problems are staged and restaged by 'spectactors' with the aim of finding solutions to oppression. These kinds of theatre that are not designed for straightforward consumption by spectators may also be seen in wider ethical terms, as imagining artistic production as a form of open social process. In all these forms of theatre, what matters, ethically and politically, is what is done with theatre itself rather than what the theatre is about. Increasingly, the relationship between theatre and ethics comes to be a question of form rather than content. It is how you make it, and what relationships you establish in the making of it (between producers, consumers, actors, spectators, participants), that matters, not what message or ideology you are trying to communicate. This focus on process and form goes hand in hand with an openness to the future and the unpredictable rather than a closure around a specific ethical position. This emphasis on openness and the establishment of space for the unknown, the unpredictable and the sheer 'otherness' of other people is typical of a reorientation in ethical thought which started to take shape in the middle of the twentieth century. In the next section the nature and cause of this reorientation are briefly explained. The book then concludes with a consideration of how theatre practice and writing about theatre have participated in this reorientation of ethical thought.

Ethics after Auschwitz

The key historical event for the late twentieth-century reorientation of ethics is the Nazi genocide. The systematic mass murder of European Jews by the National Socialist (Nazi) government of Germany under Adolf Hitler led, in the second half of the twentieth century, to a number of

fundamental reassessments of European civilisation and culture. The idea that human history involved progress towards
ever greater realisation of human potential was repudiated.
Instead of progress, the history of the first half of the twentieth century had involved a lapse into appalling depths of
human depravity. How had this happened in the midst of
a Europe that prided itself on its civilisation, the sophisti-
cation of its philosophical thought and the strength of its
collective commitment to universal humanist ideals such as
'liberty, equality, fraternity'? For many artists and thinkers in the aftermath of this event, the lapse into depravity
was no accident. It was, instead, the outcome of the very
processes, of enlightenment and modernisation, which had
initially promised to bring peace and harmony to a liberated
humanity.

This was the explanation offered by Theodor Adorno and
Max Horkheimer in *The Dialectic of Enlightenment* (1947).
For Adorno and Horkheimer, the movement of enlightenment thought and the practices that flow from it involve a
systematic attempt to secure the domination of nature –
the world – by human reason. In the attempt at complete
mastery and control over the world – enacted through the
development of technologies, the organisation of people
and the exploitation of human and natural resources in the
name of progress and prosperity – humanity (or Western
humanity) turned its own rationality into an irrational drive
to power. In seeking to subject the entire world to its control, humanity found that, in the process, it had subjected
itself to domination. Irrational and inhuman processes such

as mechanisation, first created by rational humans, assumed a logic of their own and took over. The systematic attempt to eliminate an entire people – the Jews – in what were, in effect, factories of death was a sinister and irrational outcome of the attempt to secure human domination over the world by means of processes of rational organisation.

Another thinker whose work contributed substantially to this re-evaluation of enlightenment modernity was Emmanuel Levinas. Levinas was a Jewish philosopher of Lithuanian origin who eventually, after World War Two, settled and worked in France. He was himself a prisoner of the Germans throughout World War Two, and many members of his close family were murdered by the Nazis. Levinas' answer to the question of how the Nazi genocide could have happened both resembled and differed from that offered by Adorno and Horkheimer. It was similar in that it involved a critical stance towards the heroic version of the enlightenment and its march of progress, which he described, in 'Ethics as First Philosophy' (1984), reprinted in *The Levinas Reader* (1989), as 'a miracle of modern Western freedom unhindered by any memory or remorse, and opening onto a "glittering future" where everything can be rectified' (p. 78).

Levinas' response is made at the level of philosophy, in relation to the very grounds of how Europeans had come to think about themselves and the world. His subsequent philosophical work was dedicated to rethinking precisely those relationships (between self and world) in terms radically different from those we have seen initiated by Aristotle and continued through the traditions of 'Western philosophy' by philosophers such as Kant. In particular, he replaced a philosophical emphasis on 'being' with a dedication to an ethics based on the existence of the 'other'. For Levinas, traditional philosophy had been primarily concerned with understanding what it meant to 'be' someone in the world, or, in the specific sub-field of philosophy we have come to call 'ethics', how best to 'be' in the world. In the work of Aristotle this emphasis is expressed in terms of *ethos*, and the aim of most fully realising one's potential to live a good life. In the more recent, and for Levinas politically disastrous, case of Martin Heidegger, the concern with being had become elevated into a pursuit of 'Being', in which the task of human life is the fullest and most authentic realisation of who you are. It is not difficult to see how such a philosophy could be translated into a political ideology that emphasised above all else an idea of authentic identity. For Nazi ideology the full realisation of one's identity as a German would carry with it the obligation either to subjugate or to eliminate all other possible identities. This emphasis on 'being' or 'Being' was the root of the problem. Philosophy would have to start again, without 'being'. To do so it would have to begin with the 'other'.

In place of a life lived to realise one's own goals – even if those goals might involve making other people's lives better – Levinas proposes that we ought to live life eternally in relation to the 'other'. The ground of our human existence lies in our encounter with the fact that the 'other' exists, an encounter in which we ought to recognise an infinite obligation towards that 'other'. In 'Ethics as First Philosophy',

Levinas expresses this ethical obligation as something that not only takes priority in every actual situation but actually exists prior to our self. We come into being only through this responsibility to the 'other'. The ground of our being is not our self but anyone but our self:

> Responsibility for the Other, for the naked face of the first individual to come along. A responsibility that goes beyond what I may or may not have done to the Other or whatever acts I may or may not have committed, as if I were devoted to the other man before being devoted to myself. Or more exactly, as if I had to answer for the other's death even before *being*. (*The Levinas Reader*, p. 83)

By starting from the 'other' and deriving everything from the responsibility the 'other' demands, Levinas seeks to remove the human subject from its former place at the centre of the world, the place from which the human subject had previously displaced God. Modern philosophy replaced God with the self. Levinas would replace the self with the other.

Theatre after Levinas

For theatre and performance studies the appeal of Levinas' ethics seems to derive, at least in part, from the centrality of the encounter with the 'face'. For Levinas the 'face' is never any particular face but rather the otherness of the other as it appears to us in the encounter. It carries with it, in its nakedness and vulnerability, the injunction 'Thou shalt not kill' and confers upon us an infinite responsibility – up to and including the laying down of our own life – towards the other. This account of what looks like a 'face-to-face encounter' has encouraged a consideration of the relationship between spectator and actor, audience and performance, in terms of this ethical situation. Levinas' account of the encounter with the face offers the appealing prospect of identifying theatre and performance (in which such encounters are presumed to be a central element) as a cultural practice particularly well suited to the exploration of ethics. In this way theatre can recover its cultural value as a 'moral institution'. In place of the discredited enlightenment model in which the audience gains moral and sentimental education from a night out at the civic or national theatre, we might be able to develop a model of performance as an ethical encounter, in which we come face to face with the other, in a recognition of our mutual vulnerability which encourages relationships based on openness, dialogue and a respect for difference. This represents a shift in terminology in which the theatre of moral instruction gives way to performance as ethical practice. At the end of this section I address three examples of critical writing about performance that make use of this idea.

This connection between Levinas' 'face' and performance or the theatrical relationship is both fruitful and problematic. It is fruitful because it seems to permit ways of thinking about what is going on in performance or in the theatrical relationship (between actor and spectator, for example) and about what one might make of such a relationship in theatrical practice. It is problematic because it loses, in its transfer across from Levinas' philosophy to theatre and performance, much of what is distinctive in Levinas. It removes the unknowability and anonymity of the face; it dilutes the absolute quality of the demand to infinite responsibility; it obscures the idea that the self comes into being only through this encounter with, and infinite subjection to, the other. One might argue that this is just as well and that the misappropriation of Levinas by theatre and performance studies removes from his thought precisely those elements which tend towards the impossible, the mysterious and the theological, leaving a less austere but rather more viable kind of ethics, appropriate for day-to-day use. Serious Levinasians would no doubt retort that the ethics left behind after this 'misappropriation' is simply a lazy form of mundane liberalism, in which we are wearily enjoined to be nice to each other, and is thus of no use to anyone.

Another difficulty inherent in using Levinas' ethics to think about theatre and performance is that elements of Levinas' thought seem to be profoundly hostile to the category of the aesthetic, in which we would normally locate both theatre and performance. In 'Reality and Its Shadow' (1948), for example, Levinas writes that art is 'the very event of obscuring, a descent of the night, an invasion of shadow' (*The Levinas Reader*, p. 132). It seduces its viewer into evading responsibility for the world. Only in the act of critical reflection upon art – that is to say, in the work of philosophy – can we hope to return to the real and the true, and to an ethical reckoning with the world as it is. Just as it seemed to do for Plato, ethics displaces aesthetics.

Thus it is perhaps unsurprising that the Levinasian turn in thinking about theatre (or the ethical turn in performance) involves some suspicion of the purely aesthetic, and a marked preference for work which can be demonstrated to be effective. However, the value placed upon efficacy is most usually expressed in terms of the production of social or political change. The more the work in question seems to abandon direct political or social efficacy – that is, the closer it seems to approach the condition of the aesthetic (in which it is valued for its own sake) – the more likely it is that talk of efficacy will become talk of ethics. In a sense, then, in much contemporary thinking and writing about theatre and performance, the production of ethical relationships and situations is considered preferable to the production of political effects, which are often regarded as crude propaganda on the one hand or hopelessly and naively ineffective on the other. Thus ethics displaces politics.

Let us look, finally, at three recent examples of writing about theatre and performance, each of which engages with the ethics of spectatorship. The first is from Hans-Thies Lehmann's *Postdramatic Theatre* (1999). Here Lehmann is articulating how theatre might make possible an ethical relationship between people which a media-saturated world has rendered difficult or impossible:

> The basic structure of perception mediated by media is such that there is no experience of a

connection among the individual images received but above all no connection between the receiving and sending of signs; there is no experience of a relation between address and answer. Theatre can respond to this only with a *politics of perception*, which could at the same time be called an *aesthetic of responsibility (or response-ability)*. Instead of the deceptively comforting duality of here and there, inside and outside, it can move the mutual implication of actors and spectators in the theatrical production of images into the centre and thus make visible the broken thread between personal experience and perception. Such an experience would be not only aesthetic but therein at the same time ethico-political. (pp. 185–6)

For Lehmann, there is very little theatre itself can do about what he sees as the politically malign consequences of the saturation of the world by media information. Theatre cannot intervene politically in this situation, to assist, for instance, in the destruction of global media corporations. What it can do is intervene at the level of 'perception', by activating a capacity to respond (response-ability). Where the information flows of the global media typically preclude any response (other than by means of banal and pre-programmed interactivity), theatre makes the possibility of response central to the way it functions by placing actors and spectators in the same space as each other and permitting both to understand that the production of images in the theatre is something in which they are collaborating. The global media separate our perception from our personal experience by constantly bombarding us with images which either seem to have nothing to do with our experience (fantasy films) or seem to do so but do not (reality TV). Theatre reconnects perception and experience, thus perhaps healing wounds which are both personal (psychological) and social (political).

Such a theatre might work by presenting precisely the same images as those circulating in the global media, but doing so in theatrical situations in which the audience is actively aware of its own participation in the event rather than a passive recipient of media saturation. Through this re-situating of the images – of suffering humanity, for example – theatre can awaken in its audience a feeling of ethical responsibility to the people suffering in the images. Something of this sort happens in the work of Walid Raad, whose performances often take the form of illustrated lectures, mainly about the civil war in Lebanon. In *My Neck Is Thinner Than a Hair: A History of the Car Bomb in the 1975–1991 Lebanese Wars, Volume 1: January 21, 1986* (Beirut, 2004) familiar images of car bombs are shown as part of a laptop presentation and subjected to a strange process of apparent scholarly analysis in which inconsequential details and trivial information are systematically reviewed and categorised. The cool emphasis on this emotionally insignificant detail of a familiar media image of death invites an audience to respond critically to the mode of presentation. In Q&A sessions staged after the presentation, audience members – perhaps uncertain about

Raad's own intentions – interrogate the artist as to why he has chosen to focus on such details to the exclusion of ethical and political questions of murder and death. The images of the global media are re-situated to awaken an active ethical response or sense of 'response-ability'.

Implicit in Lehmann's notion of 'response-ability' is the idea that in the act of responding to something we are also taking responsibility for it. This may not be the infinite responsibility which is the ethical demand of the Levinasian 'face'. But it seems to speak the same language. In the theatre, Lehmann suggests, that which is represented acts as a call or a demand upon the spectators. Spectators are called upon to recognise that there is a relationship between what is shown in the theatre and their own experience of the world. In responding to this call, spectators take responsibility for making what is shown part of their personal experience. The spectators are invited to do something about it.

This idea of the re-activation of the spectator is one of the key concepts of ethical thought about theatre and performance. Although it tends to be articulated today in terms of ethics rather than politics (for ethics, remember, displaces politics), it follows in a tradition which can readily be traced back through Brecht. In our second textual example, this re-activation of the spectator turns her into a witness. The following extract is from 'Marina Abramović: Witnessing Shadows', a 2004 essay by Peggy Phelan, where she discusses the artist Marina Abramović's 2002 New York installation 'The House with the Ocean View', in which the artist inhabited three raised 'rooms' in the gallery space over a period of twelve days:

> The condition of witnessing what one did not (and perhaps cannot) see is the condition of whatever age we are now entering. Whether we call this period 'the post-postmodern age' or 'the age of terrorism,' it is characterized both by an intimate reawakening to the fragility of life and a more general sense of connection to one another that exceeds simple geophysical, ideological, or cultural proximity. If Levinas is right, and the face-to-face encounter is the most crucial arena in which the ethical bond we share becomes manifest, then live theatre and performance might speak to philosophy with renewed vigor. (p. 577)

Here the relationship to Levinas is explicit. In Abramović's installation the artist lived in the gallery, moving between three adjacent spaces raised above the gallery floor. Phelan's essay is concerned with the potentially transformative consequences of a personal encounter, facilitated by Abramović's work. Abramović invites the spectator to become an active witness to the actions of the work, and in the process to experience a live encounter with the other that brings a fresh awareness of the vulnerability of the human body alongside a revived understanding of the way in which the relationships between us might preserve us all from that to which we are all vulnerable, such as pain, distress and death.

For Phelan it is not just the encounter with Abramović, as other, that counts in this situation but also the way in which this encounter brings to mind – perhaps even makes present – all those countless others who are not here, who have already suffered trauma, loss and even death. Phelan's notion of the ethical in performance may be grounded in the live co-presence of performer and spectator, but it also moves beyond that immediate situation, to suggest ways in which an ethical 'reawakening' might help us think and feel about those others we only ever encounter as images amid the media saturation – as 'shadows', in fact. Phelan implies, I think, that work such as this calls its spectators to bear witness to precisely those victims of historical traumas (such as the Nazi genocide) whose deaths have called into question the ethical basis of enlightenment modernity. Such acts of witness are part of the work of developing a post-enlightenment ethics.

My third example is from 'Coming Undone' (2001), an essay by Adrian Heathfield about the work of the Chicago-based performance group Goat Island. It is not written from the conventional scholar–observer position adopted by Lehmann and, to a certain extent, by Phelan; rather it foregrounds the author's presence as someone working from within the process of the company's work, attending rehearsals and in constant conversation with members of the company. It was published as part of a reading companion to Goat Island's *It's an Earthquake in My Heart* (dietheater Künstlerhaus, Vienna, 2001). For Goat Island, the work is an always open process, and performances are instances of a further opening of the process towards a public rather than moments of conclusion or accomplishment:

> Their aesthetic is deeply engaged with an eth-
> ics of performance. This ethics has been present
> in much of their previous work, but in *It's an
> Earthquake in My Heart* it is an explicit matter
> of content. As with their immediate contem-
> poraries such as the Wooster Group and Forced
> Entertainment their aesthetic arises from a sus-
> tained practice of living with the material with
> which they work, so that a 'final' piece takes the
> form of an organic melding of elements, a life-
> world which the performers inhabit. *Earthquake*
> is an enacted meditation on the art of living, a
> work that *does* the asking of that timeless eth-
> ical question 'How to live?'. ... Rather than as an
> origin, an initiative or a beginning, the company
> often speak of the work as a response, an answer
> to a call from elsewhere, either within or out-
> side of the self. For Goat Island making art is a
> life-practice of rehearsal – something done again
> in the hope of making it work – but also a recip-
> rocal and unending cycle of call and response,
> of gift and counter-gift between themselves, and
> between themselves and us, the spectators of
> their work. All we require is an attention to their
> echoing call and the faith, perhaps, to proffer an
> answer. (n.p.)

Goat Island seem, in Heathfield's account, to invite, in their call, a response from the spectators not so much to what the work might be about, in terms of theme and content, but to the example of the work-as-life process to which the spectators have briefly been admitted. The act of critical writing about performance is thus itself construed as an ethical response to the work, part of the 'reciprocal and unending cycle of call and response, of gift and counter-gift'. Here again the influence of Levinas might be detected, in the idea of a 'call from elsewhere' that might be from 'outside of the self'. Goat Island's life-as-work is itself an ethical response to a call, and our response-ability towards it might be to reciprocate by understanding our own life and work in ethical terms, by a repeated posing of the question 'How to live?' (or 'How shall I act?') as a question about our relationships and responsibilities to others.

What further thinking about the ethics of performance, or for that matter theatre and ethics, might these three examples leave us to do? I suggest two avenues for further thought. The first is to think about their writing, and the theatre and performance they are thinking and writing about, as part of a long historical exploration of the relationship between the political, the ethical and the aesthetic. This means not making an arbitrary separation between such categories as ancient, modern and postmodern, and recognising as a result that the ethical turn in performance is a turn with a history. This might invite us to consider carefully how one moment's ethical thought about performance might differ from another's theories of theatre as a moral institution. We might note, for example, that the pressing concerns with questions of reason and emotion seem to have disappeared in contemporary ethical thought about performance, only then to wonder whether, perhaps, this opposition might be expressed in different terms, such as theory and practice. We might start to think about current discussions about the relative values (including the ethical values) of practice and theory in light of the history of thought about thought and feeling. We might wonder whether the present tendency to value practice over theory is a new form of what ethical theorists used to call 'sentimentalism'.

The second avenue is to think about what it might mean to be there. By this I mean three things: to be there is, first, simply to be present, to attend, as at the theatre; to be there is, second, to be part of it, to participate, as in politics, for example; and finally, to be there is to be there for someone, to engage in a relationship of care or support, to accept an ethical responsibility for the other. Two key questions in relation to all three formulations would then be 'Did you have to be there?' and 'Is being there enough?' We might, again, wonder whether the injunction to be there, and then some, is another iteration of a sentimental prejudice in favour of practice, which happens in the present when you are there, and against theory, which supposedly happens in the past, when you are somehow somewhere else. For Heathfield, Phelan and Lehmann, presence matters. None of them insists that you have to be there or that any ethical value is attached to presence as such. However, there is a strong tendency in this direction in all three cases, much as there is in Levinas, at least when Levinas' 'face-to-face encounter' is taken at face value. This is clear in Phelan, for whom being in the presence of Abramović, with all that it then implies, was essential to her experience of the work and her response to it. It is clear, too, in Heathfield, for whom the act of critical writing is an ethical response to an experience of being part of the process of performance, to the process having involved his presence. Even in Lehmann, presence seems to be the condition which most readily permits the recognition of a relationship between the address and the answer, a relationship that is 'not only aesthetic' but 'ethico-political'. In none of these instances is there an explicit repudiation of the category of the aesthetic that anywhere resembles the position articulated by Levinas in 'Reality and Its Shadow', but in all three there is an expectation that the aesthetic will be a pathway towards the fully ethical. Nor is there complete repudiation of the political. Lehmann is inviting us to think about how one might organise images and our relationship to them in a political way, how we might make theatre politically rather, perhaps, than make political theatre. Phelan suggests that Abramović invites a consideration of history, memory and death that is nothing if not political in its implications. Goat Island's work models a way of living in the world that is politically responsible and engaged and calls upon its audience to think about their own engagements and responsibilities. The moment of ethical encounter in work such as that discussed by Lehmann, Phelan and Heathfield (an understanding of relationship, an assumption of witnessing, a response to a call) can thus be the basis for thought, feeling or action within the sphere of politics. Ethics does not quite displace either aesthetics or politics. Aesthetic experience becomes the condition of possibility for a particular kind of ethical relationship. The ethical relationship becomes, in its turn, the ground upon which political action might be attempted.

Conclusion

At the end of Part One, I argued that Plato's writing might be interpreted as a demand 'that theatre ought to justify itself in terms of the contribution it might make to an ethical life'. In their writing Lehmann, Phelan and Heathfield all value theatre and performance which they believe makes such a contribution. I do too. However, there is a problem. We value such work for its ethical contribution because we can recognise what that contribution might be. We can name it and understand it. We might be said to identify with it, with something in it that we recognise as our own. Something about what the work says or does matches our own sense of what we would like it to say or do, corresponds with our own sense of how we would like the world to be. We are able to respond to its call because we understand the language in which it speaks to us. Perhaps we are responding not to the 'other' in such work but to 'the same', to a reflection of our own 'self'. If that is the case, perhaps the work (of which we are part) fails to make any 'contribution' to an 'ethical life', as it might be understood by Levinas, precisely because it meets our existing expectations of what such work, and such a contribution, might be. The work that would provoke a truly ethical response, in Levinas' terms, would be that work which appeared, at least, to have no ethical ambition whatsoever. Such a work would have to confront its spectators or participants with something radically other, something that could not be assimilated by their existing understanding of the ethical. It would have to issue a demand they did not know how to answer. Thus, paradoxically, the value of such an aesthetic production would lie precisely in its not being ethical, and not in its capacity radically to challenge existing ethical understanding. To think this within the terms of Levinas' philosophy, the only aesthetic production worthy of ethical consideration would be that which Levinas himself has characterised, in 'Reality and Its Shadow', as 'the very event of obscuring, a descent of the night, an invasion of shadow' (p. 132).

In *Pezzo 0 (due)* (Centro de Arte Moderna, Lisbon, 2002), Maria Donata D'Urso is visible, naked, in low light, surrounded by an insect-like scratch and crackle of electronic sound. As she moves her limbs slowly in the subdued and tightly focused pool of light, it soon becomes impossible to make out the relationships between surfaces and volumes. The light reveals to the spectator an area of human skin, beneath which lies flesh, but what precisely lies below this particular surface cannot be determined. Is this a section of her thigh or part of her back? The work is a moving sequence of sculptural forms, all produced by a single human body, and each successive form seems to recall, half-abstractly, the human figure of classical representation, but

67

without settling into a configuration in which a full human figure becomes visible in its symmetry and organisation. The work, which lasts about half an hour, seems to combine aspects of the beauty of classical statuary with some of the fascination of the contortionist. The unmistakable intention that lies behind each successive movement of the body assures the spectator that there is a single and coherent human subject carrying out these actions, even as it remains impossible to identify a single human subject from the elements of human flesh and skin which are made visible in the performance. This effect of an apparent separation of the evidence of a human mind (intention) and the actions and organisation of a human body is profoundly unsettling as well as very beautiful. The performance appears, at least, to have no interest other than the meticulous presentation of the surfaces of the body to the light. In this regard it may be regarded as having nothing other than aesthetic content. It contains no proposition about the nature of the world, offers no narrative or dramatic encounter or anything that might solicit from an audience any ethical response. There is nothing to be ethical about here. Yet in the sheer strangeness with which it presents that most familiar of forms – the human body – it issues what one might call, in language to echo Levinas', a challenge from the place of the other. The other, in this case, is simultaneously the artist who made the work and who performs it here, readily identifiable with the name Maria Donata D'Urso, and also the disorganised body the spectator encounters, which appears, in a quietly shocking way, to be something other than a single, comprehensible human body that might be attached to the name Maria Donata D'Urso. The challenge issued by this work, from the place of the other, is to our conception of what it is to be or have a human body, and to have intentions that make it do things. The human figure, so often the luminous centre of the aesthetic experience and the presence with which the spectator may easily identify, is here shadowed and obscured in such a way as to render it utterly strange to all those human figures who sit in the dark and watch it. Without making any overt ethical claim, this piece seems to challenge the human spectator to consider what it is that allows him or her to recognise another as a fellow human.

Thus in Levinas' apparent condemnation of art and the aesthetic lies the very grounds of its ethical potential. The 'invasion of shadow' that occurs in work like Donata D'Urso's is precisely the mystification that for Levinas makes art the enemy of philosophy's search for truth and light. The logic of Levinas' position, not unlike that of Plato more than two thousand years earlier, is that an ethical work or event of art would be one which demanded a labour of critical thought for its ethical potential to be realised rather than offering within itself anything of the ethical. That is, of course, the labour that writers such as Lehmann, Phelan and Heathfield are performing and, indeed, that I have started to attempt in my account of Maria Donata D'Urso's work. If their, and my own, investments and interests in theatre and performance which might make a contribution to the ethical life are to differ from the investments expressed by enthusiasts for the theatre as a moral institution such as Lessing or for efficacious performance more generally such as Brecht, it will be because the event of theatre is approached with uncertainty, with a view to the possibility of surprise, challenge or affront. This is not a call for theatre and performance to rehearse its weary repertoire of shock tactics in the hope of eliciting an ethical response from its critics. But it is to propose that the kind of demand I have suggested Plato makes, that theatre justify itself in terms of its contribution to an ethical life, might be the very thing that prevents any theatre from meeting such a demand. Theatre's greatest ethical potential may be found precisely at the moment when theatre abandons ethics.

further reading

The topic of theatre and ethics has not been addressed directly in a single volume in English before. This list of further reading therefore offers, in addition to the works cited in the text, a range of readings which anyone interested in the topic might find useful in developing research in this area. I have chosen not to identify any specific plays or performance practices other than those described in the text, on the basis that more or less any instance of theatre or performance might be considered in terms of its ethics or the ethics of its spectators. Instead I have included a range of books and articles that might be read to extend and deepen the preliminary understanding of ethics and theatre offered here.

Reading classical Greek texts, particularly those of Plato and Aristotle, is an invaluable guide to the way in which ethics has been conceived in Europe. The best accessible introduction to the European ethical tradition is probably

Alasdair MacIntyre's *A Short History of Ethics* (2002), although his work does not address the postmodern ethics of Levinas at all. Another excellent and argumentative survey, which does consider Levinas and other postmodern ethical thought, is Terry Eagleton's *Trouble with Strangers* (2009). Seán Hand's *The Levinas Reader* (1989) is a good introduction to Levinas' philosophy and will guide readers to major works. Robert Eaglestone's *Ethical Criticism* (1998) is a valuable orientation of Levinas' thought towards literary and aesthetic questions. In addition to works cited in the text, the publications below by Dwight Conquergood, Helena Grehan, and Alan Read bear most directly on contemporary ethical issues in relation to performance. Several essays addressing questions of ethics with a particular focus on theatre spectatorship are to be found in Kelleher and Ridout's *Contemporary Theatres in Europe* (2006).

Adorno, Theodor W., and Max Horkheimer. *The Dialectic of Enlightenment*. 1947. Trans. John Cumming. London: Verso, 1997.

Aeschylus. *Aeschylus II: The Suppliant Maidens and the Persians, Seven Against Thebes and Prometheus Bound*. Trans. Seth G. Benardete and David Grene. Chicago: U of Chicago P, 1956.

Aristotle. *Poetics*. Trans. Malcolm Heath. London: Penguin, 1996.

———. *The Nicomachean Ethics*. Trans. J. A. K. Thomson. Rev. Hugh Tredinnick. London: Penguin, 2004.

Barish, Jonas. *The Antitheatrical Prejudice*. Berkeley and Los Angeles: U of California P, 1992.

Boal, Augusto. *The Theatre of the Oppressed*. London: Pluto, 2000.

Bottoms, Stephen, and Matthew Goulish, eds. *Small Acts of Repair: Performance, Ecology and Goat Island*. London and New York: Routledge, 2007.

Brecht, Bertolt. *Brecht on Theatre: The Development of an Aesthetic*. Ed. and trans. John Willett. New York: Hill and Wang, 1977.

———. *Collected Plays*. Volume 3ii. *The Mother and Six Lehrstücke*. Ed. John Willett and Ralph Mannheim. London: Methuen, 1997.

Caygill, Howard. *Levinas and the Political*. London and New York: Routledge, 2002.

Conquergood, Dwight. 'Performing as a Moral Act: Ethical Dimensions of the Ethnography of Performance.' *Literature in Performance* 5 (1985): 1–13.

Davis, Tracy C. 'Theatricality and Civil Society.' *Theatricality*. Ed. Tracy C. Davis and Thomas Postlewait. Cambridge: Cambridge UP, 2004. 127–55.

Eaglestone, Robert. *Ethical Criticism*. Edinburgh: Edinburgh UP, 1998.

Eagleton, Terry. *Trouble with Strangers: A Study of Ethics*. Oxford: Blackwell, 2009.

Grehan, Helena. *The End of Ethics? Performance Politics and War*. Spec. iss. of *Performance Paradigm* 3 (2007). 9 Jan. 2009 <http://www.performanceparadigm.net/category/journal/issue-3/>.

———. *Performance, Ethics and Spectatorship in a Global Age*. Basingstoke, UK: Palgrave Macmillan, 2009.

Halliwell, Stephen. *The Aesthetics of Mimesis: Ancient Texts and Modern Problems*. Princeton, NJ: Princeton UP, 2002.

Heathfield, Adrian. 'Coming Undone.' 2001. 16 Nov. 2008 <http://www.adrianheathfield.com/cu.pdf>.

Hume, David. *A Treatise on Human Nature: Being an Attempt to Introduce the Experimental Method of Reasoning to Moral Subjects*. Ed. Ernest Campbell Mossner. London: Penguin, 1985.

Jonson, Ben. *The Alchemist and Other Plays*. Ed. Gordon Campbell. Oxford: Oxford UP, 1995.

Kant, Immanuel. *Groundwork for the Metaphysics of Morals*. 1875. Ed. and trans. Allen W. Wood. New Haven, CT, and London: Yale UP, 2002.

Kelleher, Joe, and Nicholas Ridout, eds. *Contemporary Theatres in Europe: A Critical Companion*. London and New York: Routledge, 2006.

Lampert, F. J. *German Classical Drama: Theatre, Humanity and Nation 1750–1870*. Cambridge: Cambridge UP, 1990.

Lehmann, Hans-Thies. *Postdramatic Theatre*. 1999. Trans. Karen Jürs-Munby. London and New York: Routledge, 2006.

Lessing, Gotthold. *The Hamburg Dramaturgy*. 1767–69. Trans. Helen Zimmern. New York: Dover, 1962.

Levinas, Emmanuel. *The Levinas Reader*. Ed. Seán Hand. Oxford: Blackwell, 1989.

MacIntyre, Alasdair. *After Virtue: A Study in Moral Theory*. London: Duckworth, 1985.

————. *A Short History of Ethics: A History of Moral Philosophy from the Homeric Age to the Twentieth Century*. London and New York: Routledge, 2002.

Marx, Karl, and Friedrich Engels. *The Communist Manifesto*. 1848. Ed. Gareth Stedman Jones. London: Penguin, 2002.

Middleton, Thomas, and William Rowley. *The Changeling*. Ed. N. W.Bawcutt. Manchester: Manchester UP, 1998.

Nussbaum, Martha. *The Fragility of Goodness: Luck and Ethics in Greek Tragedy and Philosophy*. Cambridge: Cambridge UP, 1986.

Phelan, Peggy. 'Marina Abramović: Witnessing Shadows.' *Theatre Journal* 56 (2004): 569–77.

Plato. *The Republic*. Trans. Desmond Lee. London: Penguin, 2003.

Read, Alan. *Theatre & Everyday Life: An Ethics of Performance*. London and New York: Routledge, 1993.

————. *Theatre, Intimacy & Engagement: The Last Human Venue*. Basingstoke, UK: Palgrave Macmillan, 2007.

Shakespeare, William. *The Tragedy of King Lear*. Ed. Jay L. Halio. Cambridge: Cambridge UP, 2005.

Smith, Adam. *The Theory of Moral Sentiments*. Ed. Knud Haakonssen. Cambridge: Cambridge UP, 2002.

Sophocles. *The Tragedies of Sophocles, from the Greek*. Trans. Thomas Francklin. London: R. Francklin, 1759.

Steinweg, Reiner. *Das Lehrstück: Brechts Theorie einer politisch-ästhetischen Erziehung*. Stuttgart: Metzler, 1972.

Wright, Elizabeth. *Postmodern Brecht: A Re-presentation*. London and New York: Routledge, 1988.

index

Theatre& small books on theatre & everything else

NEW FOR 2010...

978-0-230-57548-6

978-0-230-57462-5

978-0-230-21871-0

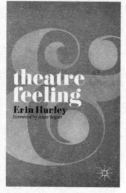

978-0-230-21846-8

978-0-230-22064-5

'Palgrave Macmillan's excellent new outward-looking, eclectic *Theatre*& series. These short books, written by leading theatre academics, do much to reintroduce some of the brightest names in theatre academia to the general reader.' - Guardian Theatre blog